Algebraic SCAT Imitation Questions:
A Fun Way to Learn Algebra

Created by Josephine Huang, Director of Math is Fun Studio LLC

Grade level 5 - 8

(1). Introduction

If you are 2nd grade to 6th grade, you must pass the School College Ability Test (SCAT) to get into a challenge summer program such as CTY at Johns Hopkins, SIG at Yale or Berkeley, or special math programs in many public schools in the United States. Here, we particularly focus on the math part of SCAT.

We found that SCAT is an interesting format of test. It requires you to differentiate among two sets of equations or problems to decide which one is greater than the other. By comparison, you not only learn to use the necessary math skills needed for the answer, but you also recognize the details of the question by reading the juxtaposition. For example, in question 1, column A is $2 \times 1 + 3 \times 2$, column B is $(2 + 1) \times (3 + 2)$. You will see that, after reading it carefully, the question wants you to pay attention to the signs: when you add first and when you multiply first. You learn that the parenthesis is a key to the answer. Numbers can be simple. With a little change of the operation signs, answers turn out very different.

From fifth grade on, you will experience imagining numbers with variables, such as x, y and z, or a and b, millions of possibilities. Let me use a simple series of questions to show you what you will be encountering on the way to Algebra:

$$(1)\ 3 + 4$$

$$(2)\ \frac{1}{3} + \frac{1}{4}$$

$$(3)\ \frac{1}{\sqrt{3}} + \frac{1}{\sqrt{4}}$$

$$(4)\ \frac{1}{a} + \frac{1}{b}$$

If you can solve (1) and (2), try to learn how to solve (3), and then, think about applying the same principle to deal with (4). There! You are aboard for Algebra: thinking with the variables! Very abstract and very fun! You are thinking like an artistic mathematician!

Let's take another example to advance our discussion further. Question 7, column A is 4n, column B is 100n. This comparison requires you to imagine possible candidates for n: if n is a positive number, even though the number is a fraction or decimal, the answer will be that 100n is greater. But if n is a negative number, no matter whether it is whole, fraction or decimal, the answer then will be that 4n is greater. Since the question does not give any restriction to what kind of number n can be, the answer is D, meaning there is not enough information to decide whether column A or B is greater. You not only learn to think with variables, but you also start to experience that an answer may not be possible!

SCAT is an interesting format for beginning learning Algebra. SCAT also has its limit for learning Algebra. You will see at the end of this practice that many of the answers to equations turn out to be like this: x = 2 or -2, y = 5 or -5. So the answer to the question would always become (D), not enough information to decide. This also shows the limit of such a format of questioning at this stage of math learning, which explains why 6th grade is the last year suitable for using SCAT. After SCAT, you go on to SAT.

We develop these questions particularly for helping 6th grade students to pass SCAT. Advanced 4th graders and 5th graders may also find this exercise useful! The question levels here go on to 8th grade and beginning 9th grade. It is a fun and challenging way to learn Algebra no matter whether you aim at the SCAT or not.

Have fun! Learn well! Wish you all the best!

(2). Directions (same as standard SCAT format)

This is what you will see on the SCAT:

Each of the following questions has two parts. One part is in Column A. The other part is in Column B. You must find out if one part is greater than the other, if the parts are equal, or if not enough information is given for you to decide. Then, choose one of the four answers below:

A) if the part in Column A is greater

B) if the part in Column B is greater

C) if the two parts are equal

D) if not enough information is given to decide

(3). Questions

Column A	Column B

1. $2 \times 1 + 3 \times 2$ $\qquad\qquad$ $(2 + 1) \times (3 + 2)$

A) if the part in Column A is greater

B) if the part in Column B is greater

C) if the two parts are equal

D) if not enough information is given to decide

2. $(6 + 5) \times (8 + 4)$ $\qquad\qquad$ $6 \times 5 + 8 \times 4$

A) if the part in Column A is greater

B) if the part in Column B is greater

C) if the two parts are equal

D) if not enough information is given to decide

3. $(17 - 9) \div (5 - 2)$ $\qquad\qquad$ $18 \div 2 - 35 \div 5$

A) if the part in Column A is greater

B) if the part in Column B is greater

C) if the two parts are equal

D) if not enough information is given to decide

Column A	Column B

4. $(16 - 2) \times 4 + 18 \div 3 - 6$ $6 + 6 \times 4 + 15 \div (9 - 8)$

A) if the part in Column A is greater

B) if the part in Column B is greater

C) if the two parts are equal

D) if not enough information is given to decide

5. $(37 + 15) \div 13 + 29 \times 100$ $196 \div 7 \times (66 + 44) - 176$

A) if the part in Column A is greater

B) if the part in Column B is greater

C) if the two parts are equal

D) if not enough information is given to decide

6. $d - 2$ $40 \div d$

A) if the part in Column A is greater

B) if the part in Column B is greater

C) if the two parts are equal

D) if not enough information is given to decide

Column A	Column B

7.   4n   100n

A) if the part in Column A is greater

B) if the part in Column B is greater

C) if the two parts are equal

D) if not enough information is given to decide

8. If X is always a positive integer, compare

         5X $X - 5$

A) if the part in Column A is greater

B) if the part in Column B is greater

C) if the two parts are equal

D) if not enough information is given to decide

9. If X is always a negative integer, compare

         10X $X - 10$

A) if the part in Column A is greater

B) if the part in Column B is greater

C) if the two parts are equal

D) if not enough information is given to decide

Column A	Column B

10. If X is always a negative integer, compare

$$10X \qquad\qquad\qquad\qquad 10 - X$$

A) if the part in Column A is greater

B) if the part in Column B is greater

C) if the two parts are equal

D) if not enough information is given to decide

11. Compare x:

$$x^2 = 100 \qquad\qquad\qquad\qquad x^2 = 99$$

A) if the part in Column A is greater

B) if the part in Column B is greater

C) if the two parts are equal

D) if not enough information is given to decide

12. If X = 2

$$X (X + 8) \times (X + 8) \qquad\qquad\qquad X \{ X [X (X + 8)] \}$$

A) if the part in Column A is greater

B) if the part in Column B is greater

C) if the two parts are equal

D) if not enough information is given to decide

Column A	Column B

13. If X = -3

$$X \, (\, X + 7 \,) \times (\, X + 7 \,)$$

$$- \, X \, [\, X \, (\, X + 7 \,) \,]$$

A) if the part in Column A is greater

B) if the part in Column B is greater

C) if the two parts are equal

D) if not enough information is given to decide

14. If X = $\frac{2}{3}$

$$\frac{X}{3} + X$$

$$\frac{X}{2} + X$$

A) if the part in Column A is greater

B) if the part in Column B is greater

C) if the two parts are equal

D) if not enough information is given to decide

Column A	Column B

15. If $X = -\dfrac{1}{5}$

$X \left(X + \dfrac{X}{5} \right) \div \left(X + \dfrac{X}{5} \right)$ $\left[X \left(X + \dfrac{X}{5} \right) \right]$

A) if the part in Column A is greater

B) if the part in Column B is greater

C) if the two parts are equal

D) if not enough information is given to decide

16. If $X = 0.75$

$X + 3 \times 7 - \dfrac{X}{3}$ $4X - \dfrac{X}{2} + 3X$

A) if the part in Column A is greater

B) if the part in Column B is greater

C) if the two parts are equal

D) if not enough information is given to decide

Column A	Column B

17. If X = - 6.25

$$[X(\frac{X}{5})] - X \qquad\qquad\qquad 100X + 100X$$

A) if the part in Column A is greater

B) if the part in Column B is greater

C) if the two parts are equal

D) if not enough information is given to decide

18. $0 \times 100{,}000$ $10 \div 0$

A) if the part in Column A is greater

B) if the part in Column B is greater

C) if the two parts are equal

D) if not enough information is given to decide (or one of the answers has no meaning)

19. $4!$ $4 \times 3 \times 2 \times 1$

A) if the part in Column A is greater

B) if the part in Column B is greater

C) if the two parts are equal

D) if not enough information is given to decide

Column A	Column B

20. $$\frac{1}{7!}$$ $$\frac{1}{9!}$$

A) if the part in Column A is greater

B) if the part in Column B is greater

C) if the two parts are equal

D) if not enough information is given to decide

21. If X = 4!

$$\frac{X\,(X+X)}{2}$$ $13X \times 2$

A) if the part in Column A is greater

B) if the part in Column B is greater

C) if the two parts are equal

D) if not enough information is given to decide

22. $\{8 \bullet [17-5 \bullet (2+1)]\,\}$ $\{4 \bullet 3 + [21-2 \bullet (8+1)]\,\} + 1$

A) if the part in Column A is greater

B) if the part in Column B is greater

C) if the two parts are equal

D) if not enough information is given to decide

Column A	Column B

23. $\{0.01 \bullet [8! - 5 \bullet (3! + 2!)]\}$ $\{2! \bullet 80 + [5! + 3! \bullet (0.75 + 3.25)]\}$

A) if the part in Column A is greater

B) if the part in Column B is greater

C) if the two parts are equal

D) if not enough information is given to decide

24. Compare the number:

   7 times a number, plus 7, is 70   100 decreased by a number,

                                                    then divided by 5, is 9

A) if the part in Column A is greater

B) if the part in Column B is greater

C) if the two parts are equal

D) if not enough information is given to decide

Column A	Column B

25. If d is always a positive integer,

the sum of 1134 and d   the product of 9 and d

A) if the part in Column A is greater

B) if the part in Column B is greater

C) if the two parts are equal

D) if not enough information is given to decide

26. $35 + (-4) - (-25)$ $24 - (-10) - (-22)$

A) if the part in Column A is greater

B) if the part in Column B is greater

C) if the two parts are equal

D) if not enough information is given to decide

27. $2.79 + (-3.55) - (-1.48)$ $0.72 - (-4.89) + (-4.93)$

A) if the part in Column A is greater

B) if the part in Column B is greater

C) if the two parts are equal

D) if not enough information is given to decide

Column A	Column B

28. $\quad \dfrac{5}{14} + \left(-\dfrac{2}{9}\right) - \left(-\dfrac{1}{3}\right)$ $\qquad\qquad\qquad$ $\dfrac{4}{7} + \left(-\dfrac{7}{8}\right) - \left(-\dfrac{3}{11}\right)$

A) if the part in Column A is greater

B) if the part in Column B is greater

C) if the two parts are equal

D) if not enough information is given to decide

29. $\quad \dfrac{3}{5} \bullet \left(-\dfrac{7}{8}\right) \bullet \left(-\dfrac{9}{11}\right)$ $\qquad\qquad$ $\dfrac{4}{5} \bullet \left(-\dfrac{2}{3}\right) \bullet \left(\dfrac{9}{10}\right)$

A) if the part in Column A is greater

B) if the part in Column B is greater

C) if the two parts are equal

D) if not enough information is given to decide

30. $\quad \dfrac{11}{10} \div \left(-\dfrac{3}{5}\right) \times \left(-\dfrac{7}{12}\right)$ $\qquad\qquad$ $\dfrac{7}{15} \times \left(-\dfrac{8}{9}\right) \div \left(-\dfrac{3}{7}\right)$

A) if the part in Column A is greater

B) if the part in Column B is greater

C) if the two parts are equal

D) if not enough information is given to decide

Column A	Column B

31.   a(3+a)+4[a-(-9)]   (a+7)+5(a+11)-(-a)

If a=7

A) if the part in Column A is greater

B) if the part in Column B is greater

C) if the two parts are equal

D) if not enough information is given to decide

32.   b-(18-b)+12[b+(-9)]   b(b+4)+2[b-(-b)]

If b=13

A) if the part in Column A is greater

B) if the part in Column B is greater

C) if the two parts are equal

D) if not enough information is given to decide

33. $5c - 2! - 3! - 2(-c)$ $c^2 + \dfrac{c}{3} - 15c$

If c=21

A) if the part in Column A is greater

B) if the part in Column B is greater

C) if the two parts are equal

D) if not enough information is given to decide

Column A	Column B

34. Compare a and b:

$196 \div a = 14$ $14 \times b = 196$

A) if the part in Column A is greater

B) if the part in Column B is greater

C) if the two parts are equal

D) if not enough information is given to decide

35. Compare a and b:

$8a + 4a = 144$ $12b - 4b + 22 = 126$

A) if the part in Column A is greater

B) if the part in Column B is greater

C) if the two parts are equal

D) if not enough information is given to decide

Column A	Column B

36. Compare a and b:

$13a - (-5) + a = 93$ $-6b \bullet (-8b) -52 = 92$

A) if the part in Column A is greater

B) if the part in Column B is greater

C) if the two parts are equal

D) if not enough information is given to decide

37. $5^{-7} \times 5^{-11}$ $5^{4} \times 5^{-20}$

A) if the part in Column A is greater

B) if the part in Column B is greater

C) if the two parts are equal

D) if not enough information is given to decide

38. $5^{13} \times 5^{-8}$ $5^{2} \div 5^{-3}$

A) if the part in Column A is greater

B) if the part in Column B is greater

C) if the two parts are equal

D) if not enough information is given to decide

Column A	Column B

39. $100^{17} \div 100^{-3}$ $100^{8} \div 100^{-13}$

A) if the part in Column A is greater

B) if the part in Column B is greater

C) if the two parts are equal

D) if not enough information is given to decide

40. $23^{-9} \div 23^{8}$ $23^{-4} \times 23^{-12}$

A) if the part in Column A is greater

B) if the part in Column B is greater

C) if the two parts are equal

D) if not enough information is given to decide

41. 8.977×10^{8} 15.988×10^{7}

A) if the part in Column A is greater

B) if the part in Column B is greater

C) if the two parts are equal

D) if not enough information is given to decide

Column A	Column B

42.　　　　　4.75×10^{-4}　　　　　　　　　　　47.5×10^{-5}

A) if the part in Column A is greater

B) if the part in Column B is greater

C) if the two parts are equal

D) if not enough information is given to decide

43. Compare t and u:

$$8t = \frac{1}{7}$$　　　　　　　　　　　　　$$6u = \frac{1}{9}$$

A) if the part in Column A is greater

B) if the part in Column B is greater

C) if the two parts are equal

D) if not enough information is given to decide

44. Compare m and n:

$$5.86 - m = 1.79$$　　　　　　　　　$$n + m = 8.14$$

A) if the part in Column A is greater

B) if the part in Column B is greater

C) if the two parts are equal

D) if not enough information is given to decide

Column A	Column B

45. Compare r and s:

$$r \times \frac{5}{9} = 20$$

$$\frac{(r+s)}{4} = 17$$

A) if the part in Column A is greater

B) if the part in Column B is greater

C) if the two parts are equal

D) if not enough information is given to decide

46. Compare y and z:

$$3 \left(y - \frac{y}{2} \right) = 9$$

$$(-z)(y - z) = 16$$

A) if the part in Column A is greater

B) if the part in Column B is greater

C) if the two parts are equal

D) if not enough information is given to decide

47. $\sqrt{289}$ $\sqrt{196}$

A) if the part in Column A is greater

B) if the part in Column B is greater

C) if the two parts are equal

D) if not enough information is given to decide

Column A	Column B

48. $\quad\sqrt{\dfrac{49}{81}}$ $\qquad\qquad\qquad$ $\sqrt{\dfrac{64}{121}}$

A) if the part in Column A is greater

B) if the part in Column B is greater

C) if the two parts are equal

D) if not enough information is given to decide

49. Compare X and Y:

$$X^2 = 144 \qquad\qquad\qquad \sqrt{Y} = 169$$

A) if the part in Column A is greater

B) if the part in Column B is greater

C) if the two parts are equal

D) if not enough information is given to decide

50. Compare X and Y:

$$X^2 = 196 \qquad\qquad\qquad Y^2 = 225$$

A) if the part in Column A is greater

B) if the part in Column B is greater

C) if the two parts are equal

D) if not enough information is given to decide

Column A	Column B

51. $\quad 7\dfrac{1}{250}$ $\qquad\qquad\qquad\qquad\qquad$ 7.004

A) if the part in Column A is greater

B) if the part in Column B is greater

C) if the two parts are equal

D) if not enough information is given to decide

52. $\quad 1.6 \times \sqrt[3]{27}$ $\qquad\qquad\qquad\qquad\qquad$ 1.5π

A) if the part in Column A is greater

B) if the part in Column B is greater

C) if the two parts are equal

D) if not enough information is given to decide

53. $\quad 7.01$ $\qquad\qquad\qquad\qquad\qquad$ $\sqrt[3]{343}$

A) if the part in Column A is greater

B) if the part in Column B is greater

C) if the two parts are equal

D) if not enough information is given to decide

Column A	Column B

54. $\dfrac{1}{\sqrt{289}}$ $\qquad\qquad$ $\dfrac{1}{\sqrt[3]{2197}}$

A) if the part in Column A is greater

B) if the part in Column B is greater

C) if the two parts are equal

D) if not enough information is given to decide

55. Turn the fractions to decimals and compare the hundredths place:

$\dfrac{7}{11}$ $\qquad\qquad$ $\dfrac{3}{16}$

A) if the part in Column A is greater

B) if the part in Column B is greater

C) if the two parts are equal

D) if not enough information is given to decide

56. Turn the fractions to decimals and compare the thousandths place:

$\dfrac{81}{99}$ $\qquad\qquad$ $\dfrac{33}{51}$

A) if the part in Column A is greater

B) if the part in Column B is greater

C) if the two parts are equal

D) if not enough information is given to decide

Column A	Column B

57. Compare n1 and n2:

$$\frac{9}{n1} = \frac{54}{84}$$

$$\frac{77}{154} = \frac{n2}{14}$$

A) if the part in Column A is greater

B) if the part in Column B is greater

C) if the two parts are equal

D) if not enough information is given to decide

58.   0.033%   0.151%

A) if the part in Column A is greater

B) if the part in Column B is greater

C) if the two parts are equal

D) if not enough information is given to decide

59.   70% of 120   120% of 70

A) if the part in Column A is greater

B) if the part in Column B is greater

C) if the two parts are equal

D) if not enough information is given to decide

Column A	Column B

60. total interest of a loan of $2000

    at the rate of 7% over $2\frac{1}{2}$ years

    (not compounded)

total interest of a loan of $3600

    at the rate of 3.5% over 3 years

    (not compounded)

A) if the part in Column A is greater

B) if the part in Column B is greater

C) if the two parts are equal

D) if not enough information is given to decide

61. total interest of a loan of $1000

    at the rate of 6.5% over 2 years

    (compounded)

total interest of a loan of $3600

    at the rate of 1.5% over $2\frac{1}{2}$ years

    (compounded)

A) if the part in Column A is greater

B) if the part in Column B is greater

C) if the two parts are equal

D) if not enough information is given to decide

Column A	Column B

62. total interest of a loan of $15,000

at the rate of 5% over $3\frac{1}{2}$ years

(not compounded)

total interest of a loan of $15,000

at the rate of 4% over 4 years

(compounded)

A) if the part in Column A is greater

B) if the part in Column B is greater

C) if the two parts are equal

D) if not enough information is given to decide

63. Compare the first year's amount of interest:

total amount of principle $2,000,

interest rate 6%, 6 years,

semi-annually (compounded)

total amount of principle $4,000,

interest rate 5.5%, 5 years,

quarterly (not compounded)

A) if the part in Column A is greater

B) if the part in Column B is greater

C) if the two parts are equal

D) if not enough information is given to decide

Column A	Column B

64. Compare the total weight:

$5\frac{3}{4}$ bags of nuts,

each bag holds $7\frac{4}{5}$ pounds

$6\frac{7}{8}$ bags of candy,

each bag holds $4\frac{2}{3}$ pounds

A) if the part in Column A is greater

B) if the part in Column B is greater

C) if the two parts are equal

D) if not enough information is given to decide

65. Compare the fraction:

$\frac{2}{5}$ of a pizza

divided into $\frac{17}{22}$ equal parts

$\frac{1}{6}$ of a pizza

divided into $\frac{4}{9}$ equal parts

A) if the part in Column A is greater

B) if the part in Column B is greater

C) if the two parts are equal

D) if not enough information is given to decide

Column A	Column B

66. if the value of a book is more than $20, which discount save more:

buy the book at 25% off and with a coupon of 10 dollars off	buy the book at 40% off and with a coupon of extra 10% off

A) if the part in Column A is greater

B) if the part in Column B is greater

C) if the two parts are equal

D) if not enough information is given to decide

67. Compare a and b:

a is four times c and c is 8% of 20	b is half of d and d is $2^3 + 5$

A) if the part in Column A is greater

B) if the part in Column B is greater

C) if the two parts are equal

D) if not enough information is given to decide

Column A	Column B

68. Compare c and d:

$$4c + 10 = 2\,(c + 12)$$ $$3d - 6 + \frac{d}{2} = 5d - 18$$

A) if the part in Column A is greater

B) if the part in Column B is greater

C) if the two parts are equal

D) if not enough information is given to decide

69. Compare e and f:

$$-e + 3e - 7 = 2e + 3e + 2$$ $$4f\,(6 - 2) = 5f + 7f - 16$$

A) if the part in Column A is greater

B) if the part in Column B is greater

C) if the two parts are equal

D) if not enough information is given to decide

70. Compare g and h:

$$3g + \frac{1}{4} = 5g$$ $$3h + 6h = 1\frac{2}{3}$$

A) if the part in Column A is greater

B) if the part in Column B is greater

C) if the two parts are equal

D) if not enough information is given to decide

Column A	Column B

71. Compare i and j:

$5i - (-3!) + i = 6i + 6$ $\qquad\qquad$ $2(9j + 2) = 10\frac{j}{2} + 13j + 7$

A) if the part in Column A is greater

B) if the part in Column B is greater

C) if the two parts are equal

D) if not enough information is given to decide

72. Compare X and Y:

$$X + 2Y = 30$$
$$2X + Y = 30$$

A) if the part in Column A is greater

B) if the part in Column B is greater

C) if the two parts are equal

D) if not enough information is given to decide

Column A	Column B

73. Compare X and Y:

$$X + 2Y = 30$$

$$2X + Y = 45$$

A) if the part in Column A is greater

B) if the part in Column B is greater

C) if the two parts are equal

D) if not enough information is given to decide

74. Compare X and Y:

$$9X + 3Y = 42$$

$$2X + 5Y = 31$$

A) if the part in Column A is greater

B) if the part in Column B is greater

C) if the two parts are equal

D) if not enough information is given to decide

Column A	Column B

75. Compare X and Y:

$$2(X+Y)=\frac{1}{8}$$

$$3X-2Y=\frac{1}{2}$$

A) if the part in Column A is greater

B) if the part in Column B is greater

C) if the two parts are equal

D) if not enough information is given to decide

76. Compare X and Y:

$$X(X-XY)=28$$

$$2X-(-5)=13$$

A) if the part in Column A is greater

B) if the part in Column B is greater

C) if the two parts are equal

D) if not enough information is given to decide

Column A	Column B

77. Compare X and Y:

$$X (X + Y) = 24$$

$$X + Y = 8$$

A) if the part in Column A is greater

B) if the part in Column B is greater

C) if the two parts are equal

D) if not enough information is given to decide

78. Compare X and Y:

$$\frac{3 (6X - 4Y)}{3} = 10$$

$$2X - \frac{Y}{2} = 10$$

A) if the part in Column A is greater

B) if the part in Column B is greater

C) if the two parts are equal

D) if not enough information is given to decide

Column A	Column B

79. Compare X and Y:

$$\frac{10\,(5X-Y)}{5!} = \frac{9}{4}$$

$$2X - 2Y = 30$$

A) if the part in Column A is greater

B) if the part in Column B is greater

C) if the two parts are equal

D) if not enough information is given to decide

80. Compare X and Y:

$$\frac{1}{7}X + \frac{3}{9}\,Y = \frac{1}{7}$$

$$6\,X - 7\,Y = 0$$

A) if the part in Column A is greater

B) if the part in Column B is greater

C) if the two parts are equal

D) if not enough information is given to decide

| Column A | Column B |

81. Compare X and Y:

$$Y = 6X - 5Y + 11$$

$$5Y = 2X - 3$$

A) if the part in Column A is greater

B) if the part in Column B is greater

C) if the two parts are equal

D) if not enough information is given to decide

82. Compare X and Y:

$$\frac{8}{13}X - 2Y = 3$$

$$\frac{3}{11}X + \frac{2}{8}Y = 4$$

A) if the part in Column A is greater

B) if the part in Column B is greater

C) if the two parts are equal

D) if not enough information is given to decide

Column A	Column B

83. Compare X and Y:

$$(X-7)^2 = 64$$

$$(Y+9)^2 = 81$$

A) if the part in Column A is greater

B) if the part in Column B is greater

C) if the two parts are equal

D) if not enough information is given to decide

84. Compare X and Y:

$$(X-11)^2 = 841$$

$$(Y-3)^2 = 961$$

A) if the part in Column A is greater

B) if the part in Column B is greater

C) if the two parts are equal

D) if not enough information is given to decide

Column A	Column B

85. Compare X and Y:

$X + 19 < -35$ $-13 + Y > -66$

A) if the part in Column A is greater

B) if the part in Column B is greater

C) if the two parts are equal

D) if not enough information is given to decide

86. Compare X and Y:

$\dfrac{X}{8} + \dfrac{4}{9} < 3$ $\dfrac{7}{12} + \dfrac{Y}{5} > 5$

A) if the part in Column A is greater

B) if the part in Column B is greater

C) if the two parts are equal

D) if not enough information is given to decide

Column A	Column B

87. $a^2 + b^2 = c^2$, Compare c^2

    if a = 7, b = 12   if a = 3, b = 16

A) if the part in Column A is greater

B) if the part in Column B is greater

C) if the two parts are equal

D) if not enough information is given to decide

88. Compare b:

    $11^2 + b^2 = 19^2$ $12^2 + b^2 = 20^2$

A) if the part in Column A is greater

B) if the part in Column B is greater

C) if the two parts are equal

D) if not enough information is given to decide

89. Compare a^2:

    $a^2 + 23^2 = 40^2$ $a^2 + 21^2 = 38^2$

A) if the part in Column A is greater

B) if the part in Column B is greater

C) if the two parts are equal

D) if not enough information is given to decide

Column A	Column B

90. Compare m:

$$m = \frac{y2-y1}{x2-x1}\text{ , 2 points can be shown as (x1, y1) and (x2, y2)}$$

(16 , 13) (11 , 7)   (14 , 8) (6 , 9)

A) if the part in Column A is greater

B) if the part in Column B is greater

C) if the two parts are equal

D) if not enough information is given to decide

91. Compare b:

$$Y = mx + b \text{ , } m = \frac{y2-y1}{x2-x1}$$

(3 , 5) (6 , 8)   (2 , 9) (4 , 5)

A) if the part in Column A is greater

B) if the part in Column B is greater

C) if the two parts are equal

D) if not enough information is given to decide

Column A	Column B

92. Compare y:

If y = 6x + 7	if $y = x^2 - 7$
x=6	x = 7
y=?	y = ?

A) if the part in Column A is greater

B) if the part in Column B is greater

C) if the two parts are equal

D) if not enough information is given to decide

93. Compare a:

Input 0 2 8	input 3 4 8
Output -1 3 a	output 5 7 a

A) if the part in Column A is greater

B) if the part in Column B is greater

C) if the two parts are equal

D) if not enough information is given to decide

Column A	Column B

94. Compare r:

Input	6	-1	0	input	10	6	r
Output	2	5	r	output	5	6	1

A) if the part in Column A is greater

B) if the part in Column B is greater

C) if the two parts are equal

D) if not enough information is given to decide

95.

Column A: $\dfrac{xy8md}{x^2y4md}$

Column B: $\dfrac{3xy2md}{x^2ymd}$

If x = -2, y = 3, m = -4, d = 5

A) if the part in Column A is greater

B) if the part in Column B is greater

C) if the two parts are equal

D) if not enough information is given to decide

Column A	Column B

96. $\dfrac{\dfrac{1}{a}}{\dfrac{a}{b}}$ $\dfrac{\dfrac{b}{ab}}{\dfrac{a}{ab}}$

if a = -3, b = -1

A) if the part in Column A is greater

B) if the part in Column B is greater

C) if the two parts are equal

D) if not enough information is given to decide

97. $\left(1 - \dfrac{b}{ab}\right)\dfrac{a}{b}$ $\dfrac{\left(1 - \dfrac{a}{ab}\right)\dfrac{1}{b}}{\dfrac{a}{b}}$

If a= 2, b = -2

A) if the part in Column A is greater

B) if the part in Column B is greater

C) if the two parts are equal

D) if not enough information is given to decide

Answer Key

1. B   2. A   3. A   4. A   5. C

6. D   7. D   8. A   9. D   10. B

11. D   12. A   13. B   14. B   15. B

16. A   17. A   18. D   19. C   20. A

21. B   22. C   23. A   24. B   25. D

26. C   27. A   28. A   29. A   30. A

31. A   32. B   33. A   34. C   35. B

36. A   37. B   38. C   39. B   40. B

41. A   42. C   43. B   44. C   45. A

46. D (Y=6, Z = -2 or 8)

47. A   48. A   49. B   50. D (X = 14 or -14, Y = 15 or -15)

51. C   52. A   53. A   54. B   55. B

56. A   57. A   58. B   59. C   60. B

61. B   62. A   63. B   64. A   65. A

66. D   67. B   68. B   69. A   70. B

71. D (i is not identifiable)

72. C   73. A   74. B   75. A

76. A   77. B (use x = 8 − y, so (8-y)(8)=24, y = 5, x = 3)

78. B   79. A   80. A

81. B   82. A   83. D (x= -1 or 15, y = 0)

84. D (x = 40 or -18, y = 34 or -27, * $29^2 = 841$, $31^2 = 961$)

85. B   86. B   87. B   88. D   89. D   90. A

91. B   92. A   93. C   94. B   95. A

96. B   97. B

*Please let me know if you have any questions or comments. Thank you!

 vertexjo@yahoo.com

Published by Math is Fun Studio LLC

~ for the love of all children

Remember to try to make up your own questions!

Think like a question designer!

Made in the USA
Columbia, SC
11 June 2024

36947141R00029